Frankenstein

Mary Shelley

TEACHER GUIDE

NOTE:

The trade book edition of the novel used to prepare this guide is found in the Novel Units catalog and on the Novel Units website. Using other editions may have varied page references.

Please note: We have assigned Interest Levels based on our knowledge of the themes and ideas of the books included in the Novel Units sets, however, please assess the appropriateness of this novel or trade book for the age level and maturity of your students prior to reading with them. You know your students best!

ISBN 978-1-56137-750-3

Copyright infringement is a violation of Federal Law.

© 2020 by Novel Units, Inc., St. Louis, MO. All rights reserved. No part of this publication may be reproduced, translated, stored in a retrieval system, or transmitted in any way or by any means (electronic, mechanical, photocopying, recording, or otherwise) without prior written permission from Novel Units, Inc.

Reproduction of any part of this publication for an entire school or for a school system, by for-profit institutions and tutoring centers, or for commercial sale is strictly prohibited.

Novel Units is a registered trademark of Conn Education.

Printed in the United States of America.

To order, contact your
local school supply store, or:

Toll-Free Fax: 877.716.7272
Phone: 888.650.4224
3901 Union Blvd., Suite 155
St. Louis, MO 63115

sales@novelunits.com
novelunits.com

Table of Contents

Plot Summary 3

Background on the Novelist 7

Initiating Activities 8
    Anticipation Guide, Viewing, Log, Verbal Scales,
Background Information on the Gothic Novel, Role
Play, Geography, Prediction, Writing, Discussion
Topics and Questions, Evidence Gathering, Book Hook,
Vocabulary

Vocabulary, Discussion Questions,
Writing Ideas, Activities
    Letters 1–4 12
    Chapters 1–4 15
    Chapters 5–7 18
    Chapters 8–11 21
    Chapters 12–15 23
    Chapters 16–19 25
    Chapters 20–22 27
    Chapters 23–24 29

Post-reading Extension Activities 31
    Discussion Questions, Further Reading and
Viewing, Writing, Listening/Speaking, Drama, Language
Study, Art, Music, Research

Plot Summary

The Letters

Letter 1: The novel opens with a letter from explorer R. Walton to his sister in England, sometime during the 1700s. Walton reports that he has arrived in St. Petersburgh (Russia) and is confident that he will succeed in finding a more direct route to the North Pole.

Letter 2: Three months later Walton writes that he has hired a ship and is gathering sailors for the voyage, but regrets that he has no friends.

Letter 3: Four months later Walton says that he is well on his way and will be careful.

Letter 4: The following month, August, Walton writes that while the ship was locked in by ice, he and his men observed a gigantic man pass northward on a dog-drawn sledge. A few hours later the ice broke and the sailors retrieved a stranger from a floating ice fragment. The stranger explained that he was pursuing a "demon"—and was eager to hear more about the giant the men had seen. As Walton and the stranger became friends over the next couple of weeks, the stranger offered to tell the tale of his own misfortunes in hopes that Walton would avoid some of the same pitfalls. The bulk of the novel is the stranger's story, recorded by Walton.

Victor Frankenstein's Story

Chapter 1: Walton's record of the stranger's story begins. His father, from a distinguished family, had married the daughter of his deceased friend. Despite the gap in ages, these two loved each other and doted on their son, Victor. When he was five, they adopted Elizabeth, a lovely girl who had been raised by a peasant family after her mother, wife of a nobleman, died in childbirth, and it became clear that her father was not coming back for Elizabeth. As the children grew up together in Switzerland, Victor quickly grew to love Elizabeth, his "more than sister."

Chapter 2: When Victor was seven, his parents had a second son. As a school-boy filled with curiosity about the physical world, Victor made one close friend—Henry Clerval. Henry's goal was to become a famous, adventurous benefactor to mankind; Victor's was to banish disease. After seeing an oak blasted by lightning, Victor became intrigued with a teacher's explanation of galvanism.

Chapter 3: After nursing Elizabeth through a bout with scarlet fever, Victor's mother caught the fever herself and died. Shortly thereafter, 17-year-old Victor went off to the university at Ingolstadt, where he became the disciple of Professor Waldman, a teacher who specialized in chemistry.

Chapter 4: During the course of his anatomy studies, Victor examined many dead bodies from charnel-houses and discovered how to bring dead matter to life. For months he was so obsessed with working on his "creation" that he failed to write or visit his family.

Chapter 5: One November night, after two years of working on the creature, he succeeded in bringing it to life—and was immediately filled with horror and disgust. He rushed to his room, fell into a fitful sleep, then escaped to the courtyard after the monster came in and held up the curtain around his bed. In the morning he walked the streets until his friend Clerval—who had just come to the University to study Oriental languages—happened to find him. Overjoyed to find that the monster appeared to have left the apartment, Frankenstein fell into a nervous fever and was bedridden for months while Clerval nursed him back to health.

Chapter 6: Clerval gave Victor a letter from Elizabeth with news about the family. Victor's brother Ernest was now 16 and planning to enter the foreign service. Justine—a devoted servant who had lived with the family since age 12 and cared for Victor's mother through her final illness—had grown clever, gentle, and pretty. Victor's youngest brother, dimpled curly-haired William, had acquired a couple of little girlfriends. After several more months of recuperation, during which Victor had shown Clerval around the university, Victor joyously prepared to return home to Geneva.

Chapter 7: Victor received a letter from his father with the terrible news that young William had been murdered and Victor realized at once that this was the work of the monster he had created. Returning home after an absence of six years, Victor discovered that Justine Moritz stood accused of the crime because a locket with a picture of Victor's mother—which William had begged to wear—had been found in her pocket.

Chapter 8: Although innocent, Justine confessed in order to obtain absolution from the priest, and was hanged despite the protestations of Victor and Elizabeth.

Chapter 9: Two months after Justine's death, Victor tried to cope with his despair by riding to the valley of Chamounix, a place he visited frequently as a boy.

Chapter 10: Victor descended upon a glacier and was horrified to see the monster approaching him. Frankenstein sprung on him ineffectually in an attempt to "extinguish the spark" he had created. The monster promised that he would leave Frankenstein and his loved ones alone if the scientist listened to his tale and agreed to do what the monster asked. Victor agreed to listen. (The creature's tale is told in Chapters 11-16.)

Chapter 11: The monster described his first memories of opening his eyes and wandering in the forest near Ingolstadt. When he entered a cottage one day looking for food, the villagers chased him and threw stones at him. He sought refuge in a hovel from which he could observe the comings and goings of a kind family, the De Laceys. He was especially moved by the blind old man's guitar-playing.

Chapter 12: The creature tried to help the family by gathering wood during the night. By watching them unobserved, he learned to speak.

Chapter 13: The creature learned to read by listening and watching as Felix instructed a beautiful Arab woman he loved, Safie. As he learned about family relationships and love, the creature felt his own lack of friends and relations.

Chapter 14: The creature discovered that the family had lost their fortune because of Safie's father, a conniving Turkish merchant who had been sentenced to death in France. After a sympathetic but misguided Felix had secured his escape, with the promise of Safie as his wife, the merchant betrayed Felix by telling his daughter to forget Felix. Safie, however, followed her lover and his family to Germany.

Chapter 15: The monster was now able to read the papers he had found in the pocket of the coat he took from the laboratory on his first day of life. He realized that even his creator found him hideous. One day while the younger family members were away, the creature decided to see if the family would accept him. He introduced himself to the blind man but—reassured though he was by the old man's gracious reception—found his worst fears realized when Felix, Safie, and Agatha returned home. Thinking he was protecting his father, Felix attacked the creature, who escaped to his hovel.

Chapter 16: Anguished, the creature wandered in the wood, then decided to return to the cottage and try to win back the old man. However, he overheard Felix tell the landlord that the father's life was in danger and the family was leaving forever. For the first time, the creature experienced a desire for revenge. Enraged, he burned the empty cottage that night and went in search of his creator. When he rescued a young girl from drowning—and was shot in the shoulder for his trouble—his desire for revenge deepened. He reached Geneva and happened to come upon Frankenstein's little brother. The creature tried to befriend him, but the boy's screaming enraged him and he strangled the child, his first victim.

Chapter 17: The creature demanded that Frankenstein create a female, and the scientist refused at first, but then relented when the creature appealed to his sense of guilt ("As my maker you owe me some happiness…"), promising to disappear forever to the wildest parts of South America as soon as he had a bride.

Chapter 18: Frankenstein returned from Chamounix to Geneva and procrastinated for several months. Finally, after reassuring his father that he planned to marry Elizabeth, Frankenstein headed back to England to confront the dreaded task of making a female creature. Elizabeth and Frankenstein's father had arranged some company for Frankenstein; Clerval joined him in Strasbourg and the two friends descended the Rhine by boat.

Chapter 19: For several months the friends traveled together (Windsor, Oxford, Matlock, Edinburgh) and Frankenstein worried that the creature might harm his relatives in Switzerland or follow Frankenstein and wreak vengeance on his friend, Clerval. Frankenstein convinced Clerval to leave him alone for a month or two, with the intention of creating the female monster. He rented a hut in Scotland and set up a laboratory there.

Chapter 20: Three years had passed since Frankenstein made the first creature. As he worked on the female, he began to have serious qualms about the project. What if these two hated each other? What if they created a race of fiends? When Frankenstein saw the creature looking in the window, the scientist suddenly tore the work-in-progress to pieces. Enraged, the creature warned Frankenstein, "I will be with you on your wedding-night." The next day Frankenstein received a letter from Clerval suggesting that the two meet in Perth. The following day he packed up his laboratory and sailed off, casting a basket containing the remains of the half-finished creature into the sea. After fighting a storm at sea and finally making a landing in Ireland, a crowd of residents accused Frankenstein of murder.

Chapter 21: A strangled corpse had been found on shore. Witnesses had seen a man in a boat—Frankenstein's boat—near the scene of the murder. When Frankenstein learned that the corpse was Clerval's, he fell into a fever for two months. He awoke in a jail, tended by an indifferent old woman. He won the sympathy of Mr. Kirwin, the magistrate, and was finally freed and allowed to return to Geneva.

Chapter 22: Frankenstein told his father that he felt responsible for the deaths of William, Justine, and Henry—but not why. While in Paris, he received a letter from Elizabeth, asking if he had fallen in love with someone else. He resolved to marry Elizabeth soon, assuming that the monster would kill him on his wedding night and cease his horrible vengeance. He promised in a letter to explain his misery to her on the day after the wedding. He returned home, the ceremony was performed, and the couple set sail on their honeymoon.

Chapter 23: That night Frankenstein grew agitated and asked his wife to retire. While searching for his adversary, he heard Elizabeth's scream and found her dead on the bed, with bruises on her neck. Looking up for a moment he saw the grinning monster at the window and fired his pistol, but missed. Fearful for his father's and brother's safety, Frankenstein returned to Geneva. A few days later the grief-stricken Frankenstein Senior died in his son's arms. In order to get help in tracking down the monster, the scientist told a criminal judge the whole story, but the judge did not believe him.

Chapter 24: Frankenstein traveled the globe, bent on revenge, following clues that the creature sometimes deliberately left behind. Finally, while tracking the creature across the frozen northland, Frankenstein was left drifting on a piece of ice. Here he was picked up by Walton's crew. At the end of Frankenstein's narrative, as recorded by Walton, Victor asks his new friend to kill the monster if the creature should appear after Frankenstein's death.

Final Letters: In a letter to his sister—enclosed along with Frankenstein's story—Walton describes how the ship has become surrounded by ice. The men have asked Walton to promise that he will head home—not into further danger—if the ship is freed. Frankenstein, near death, has exhorted the men not to give in to defeat. A few days later Walton writes that he has lost his friend and is returning home, his hopes blasted. He describes rising to check out a hoarse cry. He continues the letter with a description of the "wonderful catastrophe" he has just witnessed: The grief-stricken creature was leaning over his creator's coffin, begging his forgiveness. When confronted, the creature told Walton how miserable he felt and how much he hated himself. He promised to go to the far north and consign himself to ashes, then disappeared out the cabin window and was borne away on an ice raft.

Background on the Novelist

Mary Wollestonecraft Godwin (1797-1851) was no stranger to personal tragedy. Her mother, a prominent early feminist, died while giving birth to Mary and it is said that Mary perceived herself as her mother's murderer. She passed many hours at her mother's tomb, communing with her spirit and reading.

Her family was "dysfunctional" by today's standards: Her father was a pompous and aloof philosopher/writer. Her stepmother apparently despised her. Mary was never very close to her step-siblings and half-siblings; one half-sister committed suicide. She spent a lot of her girlhood in Scotland (a setting which figures in her novel), studying and reading while visiting relatives there. At 16 she ran off with the poet, Shelley (who at 21 was already famous, already a father, and already an unhappy husband). Shelley's wife Harriet then drowned herself and her unborn child. Mary and Shelley had three children: One died before she reached her first birthday, one died suddenly while still a toddler, the third—Percy—survived.

Mary wrote *Frankenstein* when she was only in her early 20's and living with Shelley in Italy (and while both were spending a lot of time with their friend, Byron). Beginning with her baby girl's death in 1818 and her beloved little William's death in 1819, Mary began to sink into depression.

To make matters worse, Shelley developed a wandering eye (for Emilia Viviani) and then drowned in 1822. Over the next 30 years Mary did a lot of writing (but none of these works achieved the acclaim of *Frankenstein)* and was courted by several men, supposedly including Washington Irving—but she turned them all down, and is quoted as saying, "I want to be Mary Shelley on my tombstone."

Initiating Activities

Choose one or more of the following activities to help students relate their background experience and knowledge to the novel.

1. **Anticipation Guide** *(See Novel Units Student Packet Activity #1)* Students discuss their opinions of statements which tap themes they will meet in the story. For example:
    a) As technology advances, most of our problems will be solved.
    b) Scientists have made the world a better place.
    c) Scientists should be given more freedom to perform experiments as they see fit.
    d) A scientist's job is to discover; s(he) is not responsible for how those discoveries are put to use.

2. **Video:** View one of the many movie versions of the story. Two that are highly recommended: the new Columbia Tri-Star video of Kenneth Branagh's *Mary Shelley's Frankenstein* and the freely-adapted classic 1931 production starring Boris Karloff.

3. **Log:** Have students keep a response log as they read. In one type of log, the student assumes the persona of one of the characters. Writing on one side of each piece of paper, the student writes in the first person ("I...") about his/her reactions to one episode in that chapter. A partner (or the teacher) responds to these writings on the other side of the paper, as if talking to the character.

    In another type of response journal, the dual entry log, students jot down brief summaries and reactions to each section of the novel as they read. The first entry could be made based on a preview of the novel—a glance at the cover and a flip through the book.

Pages	Summary	Reactions
		These might begin: "The way this story starts with a letter reminds me of another story...," "If I were Frankenstein, I wouldn't...," "I wonder why Justine...," "I like the way Shelley describes...," "I disagree with Elizabeth..."

    Also, students might simply record reactions to the story on sticky-notes placed on pertinent pages for later reference in group discussion or writing.

4. **Verbal Scales:** After students finish a section of the story, have them chart their feelings and judgments about various characters and situations using the following scales or others you construct. Students should discuss their ratings, using evidence from the story.

Like	1 2 3 4 5 6	Dislike
Happy	1 2 3 4 5 6	Sad
Active	1 2 3 4 5 6	Passive
Honest	1 2 3 4 5 6	Dishonest
Caring	1 2 3 4 5 6	Unkind
Responsible	1 2 3 4 5 6	Irresponsible
Proud	1 2 3 4 5 6	Humble
Concern for others	1 2 3 4 5 6	Self-absorbed
Pure	1 2 3 4 5 6	Corrupt
Forgiving	1 2 3 4 5 6	Vengeful
How horrifying?	1 2 3 4 5 6 7 8 9 10	
How moralistic?	1 2 3 4 5 6 7 8 9 10	
How realistic?	1 2 3 4 5 6 7 8 9 10	

5. **Background Information:** Have students research the definition of a gothic novel or provide the following information to them:

   Gothic Novel—style of horror fiction popular during the late 18th century and early 19th century that often had historical and picturesque settings; a mysterious and gloomy atmosphere; supernatural, violent events.

   Brainstorming: Write the phrase "GOTHIC NOVEL" on the board and have students generate associations they have with that phrase. Jot their ideas around the word and help them "cluster" the ideas into categories. A sample framework is shown below.

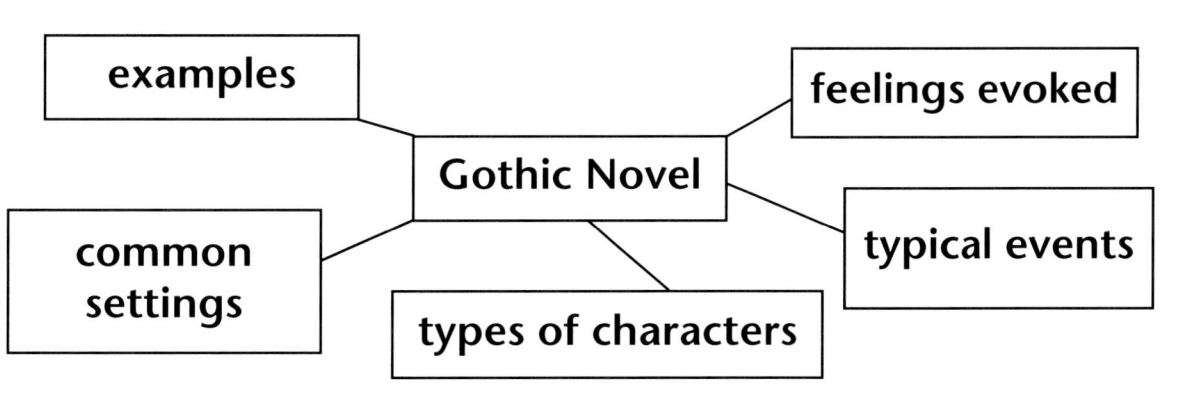

6. **Role Play:** Have small groups of students improvise skits around one of these situations (like events in the story):
   a) You are leading a group of explorers on Mars. Try to convince the mutinous group that they should risk their lives to find out what is at the bottom of a crater.
   b) You have a severe facial disfigurement; your appearance is always the first thing to which strangers react. Talk aloud about how your appearance affects your ability to make friends—and what you plan to do about it.
   c) Someone tells you if you'll do what s(he) says s(he) won't bother you any more. It's something you really don't want to do.

7. **Geography:** Have students examine a map showing the general setting of the story (Europe). Have them locate specific towns depicted or mentioned in the story (St. Petersburgh, Geneva, Ingolstadt, Edinburgh, Rhine River, Chamonix).

8. **Prediction:**
   a) Have students brainstorm a list of all the "elements" that might be found in a horror story (e.g., ghosts, insanity, mad scientists, coffins). Have them predict which ones they will find in *Frankenstein*.
   b) After students have glanced at the title and cover picture, ask—What sort of story is this? What sort of man is the man on the cover? What is your image of "Frankenstein"—from movies, TV shows, spoofs? What do you know about the monster's appearance? the reason he was created? the reason he killed people? What differences do you expect to find between these popular versions and the novel you are about to read?

9. **Prereading Journal Entries:** Freewrite for ten minutes, using one of the following "starters:"
   a) Frankenstein…
   b) In my nightmare…
   c) It was a nightmare-come-true the day I…
   d) A monster…
   e) The most horrible thing that ever happened to me…
   f) I am afraid…
   g) The difference between fear and disgust…
   h) If I could live forever…
   i) One time I was so involved in _____ that I couldn't think of anything else for days…

10. **Discussion Topics and Questions**

    Fear: What sorts of fears do people have? What are you afraid of? Why do people enjoy doing things that frighten them (e.g., going on a roller coaster ride, watching a horror movie)?

    Science: What are some problems that science has solved? What are some problems that technological advance has caused? What are some ethical issues that have arisen around scientific discoveries and inventions—like, say, nuclear fusion? What sorts of limits do we put on scientific experimentation? Should the government scrutinize scientists' experiments more closely—or allow more freedom? What does the phrase "medical ethics" mean? What are some of the ethical questions that have come up surrounding medical research? What is your opinion, for example, of using fetal tissue in research? of transplanting animal organs such as hearts and livers into humans? of "test-tube babies"?

    Parenthood: Once a parent has a child, what are his or her responsibilities to that child? What are the child's basic needs just to survive? What else does the child need to be happy? What are a parent's legal responsibilities toward a teenager? What happens if the teenager gets into trouble? Is the parent legally responsible? What do you think a parent should do about a teenager who is "out of control"—say, getting into trouble with the police? What should a parent do about a teenager who is a danger to other people?

    Deformity: What problems are faced by a person who has a physical deformity? Have you ever seen others taunt or avoid someone who is physically different? How do you explain their reactions?

11. Tell students to pay attention as they read to how they feel toward the scientist and his creation. Have them mark places where they feel sorry for the character with an **S**, and places where they pity the creature with a **P**. Students can refer to these notes during post-reading discussion and writing about the tragic happenings in the book—and who is at fault.

12. Tell students to pay attention as they read to examples of "goodness" and "evil." Have them mark places where evil is stronger than good and places where good is stronger than evil. They can refer to these notes during post-reading discussion and writing about one of the story's main themes—corruption.

13. Read a short horror story to the class to "set the mood" for *Frankenstein* (e.g., Poe's "The Telltale Heart"). After reading the novel, students might discuss similarities they noted in the content and effect of the short story.

14. **"Book Hook":** Read pp. 36–37 aloud to students ("One of the phenomena which had peculiarly attracted my attention…that I alone should be reserved to discover so astonishing a secret.") Have them discuss what the passage tells them about the characters and have them write down what questions the passage raises in their minds. Tell them to keep these questions in mind as they read the novel.

15. **Vocabulary:** Give students the following word list—

apparition	sepulchre	citadel
alchemists	dirge	scourge
purloined	viands	vagabond
portmanteau	tenement	precipices
persecutor	grovel	amphitheatre

Have students label each word with their guess as to whether the word refers to a PERSON, a PLACE, an ACTIVITY, or an OBJECT. If they have any idea what the word means, tell them to write their DEFINITION, then tell them to read on and see how the word is used in the novel.

Vocabulary • Discussion Questions
Writing Ideas • Activities

Letters 1–4

Vocabulary

forebodings	fervent	desolation	habitable
celestial	satiate	conjectures	requisite
injunction	effusions	niche	consecrated
whaler	entreated	fluctuate	fortitude
sledges	encompassed	dejection	capacious
dauntless	mariner	suppliant	wavering
embarkation	albatross	gales	prudent
compassed	apparition	capitulated	animation
benevolence	countenance	impertinent	animated
conciliating	minute	dominion	draught
paroxysm	repose	tyranny	fastidious
ameliorate	irrevocably	imperatively	lineaments

Vocabulary Activities
Some suggested activities to use with selected words from this and other vocabulary lists follow:

1. Word mapping is an activity that can be used with any vocabulary list. Students work independently or in small groups to "map" words using the framework on page 13. For words that have no antonyms, students provide a picture or symbol that captures the word meaning.

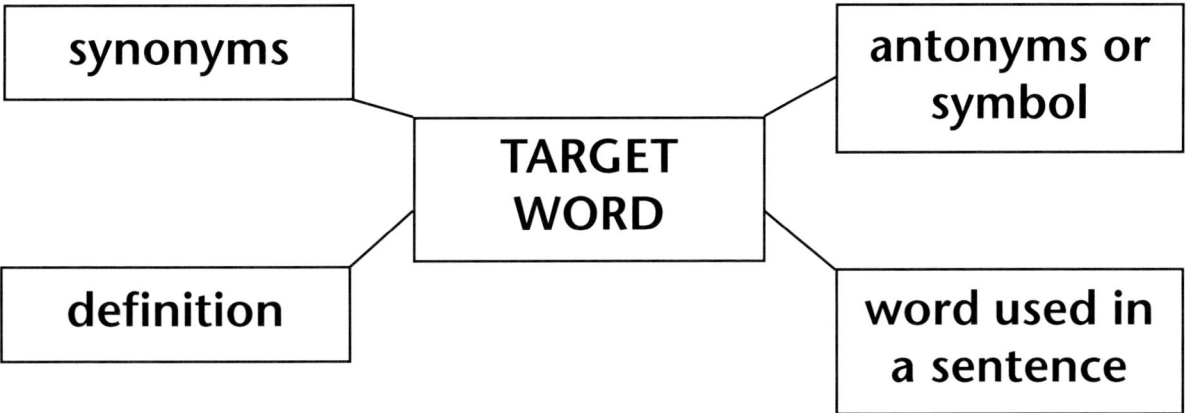

2. Have students solve analogies using words from the list and create their own. *Sample:* RIPPLES are to BREAKERS as BREEZES are to _____. *(GALES)*
3. Create a crossword puzzle with the vocabulary words. (Students might be encouraged to create their own using a puzzle-maker piece of software.)
4. Create "Jeopardy"-like statements for each word and have classmates compete to come up with the correct question. (Sample: Statement—"This word can refer either to time or size, depending on which syllable is accented." Answer—"What is **minute**?")
5. Have students create a picture puzzle for each word. On one side of a card goes a drawing or cutout that represents the word. The player tries to guess the word (printed on the other side).
6. For each vocabulary word, read the sentence in which the word is used. Have students guess what the word means, based on the context. They should explain how they arrived at their guess—then look up the definition.

A Note About Vocabulary
The word lists in this Teacher's Guide are more extensive than lists used for hands-on vocabulary activities in the Novel Units Student Packet for this title. You may find it most practical to use the lists in this guide as a reference to words which will probably require clarification during read-aloud sessions and class discussion.

Discussion Questions
1. Who is writing these four letters? *(Walton)* to whom? *(his sister)* Why? *(to describe his journey)* What kind of person is the writer? *(well-educated, adventurous, introspective)*
2. In what setting does the story begin?

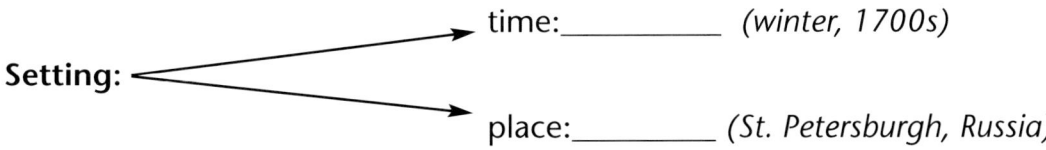

What mood does this setting help create? *(cold, barren, forbidding)*

3. Walton tells his sister that "nothing contributes so much to tranquillize the mind as a steady purpose" (p. 2). What is he feeling? *(enthusiasm, fixation on his goal)* Have you ever experienced that feeling?

4. What is Walton's goal in making this trip? *(find a route to the North Pole)* Why does he want to do this? *(He wants to break new ground, add to mankind's knowledge.)* How did his dream begin in childhood? *(He read his uncle's books about explorers.)* Do you still have dreams for the future that you developed in childhood?

5. What is your opinion of Walton's trip? Do you think he is trying something admirable—or foolish? What do you suppose his sister thinks? *(She apparently was reluctant for him to go, worried that the trip would be dangerous.)*

6. How has Walton prepared for this trip? *(For six years, he worked on his physical fitness, went on whaling trips, studied math, science, and medicine.)* What plans has he made? *(He'll hire a ship in St. Petersburgh, recruit sailors, leave in June.)* Do you think he will succeed?

7. Why does Walton want a friend? *(lonely, wants someone to share ideas, disappointments, joys with)* What sort of friend does he want? *(gentle, cultivated mind)* Are those the qualities you look for in a friend? Would you be a friend of his?

8. What does Walton think of his crew? *(admires them)* What qualities was he looking for when he selected them? *(courage, enterprise, good disposition)* Are these the criteria you would use in selecting a crew for a dangerous voyage? What do you suppose they think of him?

9. What span of time do the letters cover? *(about eight months)* Do you detect any changes in Walton's tone, as time goes on? *(enthusiasm to loneliness to fear to delight in his new friend)*

10. What is the "strange accident" that Walton writes his sister about? *(When his boat was trapped by ice, the men rescued a half-dead stranger on an ice floe.)* How does he help the stranger? *(His men warm the stranger, give him soup.)* How does he feel toward the stranger? *(curious, affectionate)* Why does the stranger decide to tell Walton the tale of his own misfortune? *(He feels that Walton is seeking knowledge, as the stranger was—and perhaps his story will teach Walton something.)*

Prediction
What will the stranger's narrative be about? The captain writes to his sister that he will someday read the manuscript "with…interest and sympathy" (p.16). How do you think he will feel about the stranger when the stranger is done with his tale?

Writing Activity
You are Captain Walton's sister. Write a letter in answer to one of his.

The Author's Craft: Framework Story
Explain that a **framework story** is a story within a story—a convention used in such classical writing as *Arabian Nights* and *Canterbury Tales*. The framework may or may not have a plot, itself, and the story may or may not return to the frame situation at the end. Ask students how

the four letters with which *Frankenstein* opens set up a story-within-a-story. *(The captain is about to share with his sister the story that the stranger has been telling him.)* Ask whether the framework has a plot. *(It does; the captain is trying to find a route to the North Pole and has met up with the scientist.)* Tell students to read on and see how *Frankenstein* actually becomes a story-within-a-story-within-a-story. *(At one point, the captain is telling his sister the story that Victor is telling him about the story that the creature told Victor.)* Tell students to watch for whether this story returns to the frame situation at the end. *(It does; we learn that the captain and his men are returning home. The captain writes several more letters to his sister.)*

Geography
Trace on a map the route that Walton plans to take through Russia across the seas, returning to England by way of the most Southern cape of Africa or South America.

Chapters 1–4

Vocabulary

syndics	deplored	sustenance	rankling
plaited	pittance	subsistence	interment
recompensing	disconsolate	penury	chamois
rustic	reverential	fervently	masquerades
sepulchre	infidels	caprice	filial
indiscriminately	metaphysical	beneficence	ignoble
predilection	inclemency	chimerical	tyros
mpediments	citadel	repined	diligence
elixir	incantations	slough	multifarious
galvanism	despicable	progeny	abortive
ligaments	ineffectual	potent	immutable
omen	malignity	prognosticated	benignity
rent	sacrilege	deferred	respite
commerce	entreaties	chaise	invincible
repugnance	repent	omnipotent	uncouth
alchemists	imbibed	procure	reprobated
repulsive	chimeras	grandeur	recapitulation
cursory	panegyric	transmuted	crucible
palpable	mien	affability	indefatigable
affection	deference	disciple	physiognomy
dogmatism	pedantry	abstruse	protracted
physiology	supernatural	irksome	charnel-houses
minutiae	generation	precepts	exalted
impracticability	acuteness	profane	vintage
procrastinate	transitory	alloy	incipient

Discussion Questions

1. What was Victor's childhood like? *(happy; father was well-respected, married a younger woman; parents traveled with him a lot, were affectionate with him and each other)* Do you see any similarities between Victor and Walton? *(Both were close to their sisters, had an eager desire to learn)*

2. How did Victor happen to be brought up with Elizabeth? *(Her mother had died in childbirth and she was being raised by peasants until Victor's parents adopted her.)* What was she like? *(blond, sensitive, kind)* What was their relationship like? *(close—Victor calls Elizabeth his "more than sister")*

3. Who is Henry Clerval? *(Victor's best friend)* What words and phrases would you use to describe him? *(talented, imaginative, adventurous, romantic, humane)*

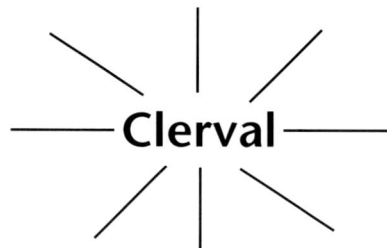

Why do you suppose he and Victor became friends? *(Both had a sense of adventure, sharp minds.)* How were they different? *(Victor was interested in science and the metaphysical; Clerval was interested in morality, languages, the humanities.)*

4. How did Victor react when he first read the writings of Agrippa? *(bored, then fascinated)* What do you suppose Agrippa was saying? How did Victor's father feel about Agrippa? *("sad trash")* Victor says that his father might have prevented "the fatal impulse that led to my ruin" (p. 25). Do you think Victor is blaming his father? What cause-and-effect chain leads to the "utter and terrible destruction" to which Victor alludes?

1._____	2._____	3._____	4._____
Cause	**Effect/Cause**	**Effect/Cause**	**Effect**
(Victor is excited about Agrippa's theories and tells his father.)	*(His father calls Agrippa's ideas "trash" but doesn't explain that they are unscientific.)*	*(Victor isn't convinced and continues to read.)*	*(These writings somehow misguide him.)*

5. How did Victor's mother die? *(nursed Elizabeth through scarlet fever, grew sick herself)* Do you think he blames Elizabeth?

6. Why did Victor go to Ingolstadt? *(parents thought that he should get more of an international education)* How does he feel about leaving his home and loved ones? *(sad to leave them but eager to see the world)* Would you feel that way if you were going off to college or a job after graduation from high school?

7. How did Victor feel about his teacher, M. Krempe? Why? *(He disliked Krempe, who told him he had been wasting his time on Magnus and Paracelsus.)* Have you ever felt about one of your teachers as Victor felt about M. Waldman? *(admired him, felt in him a soul-mate)*

8. Why did Victor like science so much? *(felt that unlike other subjects, it offered the chance to be an innovator)* Do you feel the same way? What area of science particularly intrigued him? *(structure of the human body)* Where did he do most of his work? *(graveyards, vaults, dissecting room, slaughterhouse)*

9. What discovery did Victor make? *(how to animate lifeless matter)* What advantages did Victor foresee for his discovery? *(Creating a new species would be a scientific breakthrough; creations would be grateful; death wouldn't have to be permanent.)* What cons do you foresee?

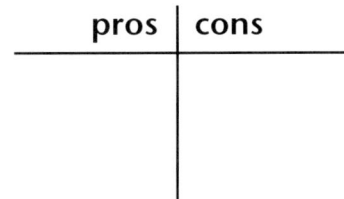

10. Why was Victor's father displeased? *(didn't hear from his son for months)* Why didn't Victor write or visit home? *(engrossed in his work; didn't want to be distracted)* How did he feel about that time, looking back on it? *(He later came to believe that you shouldn't allow your studies to weaken your affections or diminish your taste for simple pleasures.)* Do you agree with him that "no man [should allow] any pursuit whatsoever to interfere with the tranquillity of his domestic affections" (p. 40)? Do you think the great discoveries, inventions, and artistic triumphs would have occurred if this rule had been followed?

Prediction
What sort of "creation" is Victor making? Will Victor become less of a "wreck" when his creation is complete? Will Victor's father learn of the creation? Will the captain "learn from [Victor] …how dangerous is the acquirement of knowledge" (p. 38)?

Research
a) Find out who Paracelsus and Albertus Magnus were. *(Paracelsus—Swiss physician and alchemist interested in chemical remedies for physical and mental disease; Magnus—German theologian)*

b) Figure out what Victor means when he says that he learned a lesson that could have kept Greece from being enslaved, could have helped Caesar spare his country, could have kept the empires of Mexico and Peru from being destroyed by explorers.

Writing Activity
Research the allusion to the "Arabian who had been buried with the dead and found a passage to life, aided only by one glimmering and seemingly ineffectual light" (p. 37).
   a) Summarize your findings, explaining why Victor compares his feelings about the discovery to the Arabian's discovery of a passage.
   OR
   b) Describe how you once felt when, after a lot of painful effort, you finally achieved your goal.

The Author's Craft: Theme
Explain that the **theme** of a novel is the most important idea in the story. It is often about the way people deal with problems in life. What characters in a story learn is often a clue to the theme. The title and comments made by particular characters also offer clues to the theme.

Victor tells the captain to "learn from me". What has Victor learned? What do you think Shelley's "message" is, here? *(Victor has learned that knowledge and lack of humility can be dangerous.)*

Chapters 5–7

Vocabulary

infuse	convulsive	catastrophe	delineate
dun-white	lassitude	shroud	detain
demoniacal	palpitation	languor	porter
asylum	incredulous	spectre	unremitting
pertinacity	convalescence	allude	mercenary
benevolent	odious	fetter	immutable
perversity	monarchies	dissipate	vacillating
entreat	antipathy	discerning	docile
encomiums	diffident	eulogy	retarded
dilatoriness	acceded	fortnight	perambulations
salubrious	verdant	invincible	callous
livid	festering	cabriolet	slackened
placid	obscurely	environs	league
pitchy	tempest	dirge	conception
impenetrable	precipices	indelible	garb
rustic	alleviate	depravity	acquittal

Discussion Questions

1. How long did Victor work on his creation? *(two years)* How did he feel when he saw the creature's eyes open? *(horrified, disgusted)* How did he spend the night? *(pacing in his bedroom, sleeping fitfully, dreaming of Elizabeth; the creature held up the curtain by his bed and Victor ran to the courtyard where he spent the rest of the night)*

2. How do you imagine the creature, based on the description? How is this similar to/different from the popular image we have of Frankenstein's monster? *(Shelley's creature has flowing black hair, yellow eyes; the "monster movie" version has stitches in his face, straight, dead-looking hair, greenish skin.)*

As described by Shelley	As we commonly picture him

3. Why did Clerval come to Ingolstadt? *(convinced his father to let him study there)* How does Victor feel about seeing him? *(delighted)* Does he confide in his friend? *(not directly; While sick, Victor raved about the monster.)*

4. Why was Frankenstein confined for several months? *(collapsed in a nervous fever)* What do you suppose the present-day diagnosis for his condition might be? What do you suppose would have happened to Frankenstein if his friend hadn't been there during his illness? *(He believes he would have died.)*

5. How did Justine enter Frankenstein's family? *(Her widowed mother abused her from an early age; Victor's mother saw this and asked that Justine be allowed to live with her family; Justine grew up as a member of Victor's family, attended Victor's mother during her fatal illness; her siblings all died; her mother called her home, then accused her of being responsible for her siblings' deaths; mother died and Justine returned to live with Victor's family.)* How does the reader learn all this? *(Elizabeth outlines it in a letter to Victor.)* What sort of life has she had? Do you think she has had more misfortune than the author, Mary Shelley, had in real life?

6. How did Victor's interests change after his illness? *(detested natural philosophy)* How did his teachers unknowingly "torture" him when he returned to school? *(kept praising his progress in the sciences)*

7. What did Clerval study? *(Oriental languages)* Why? *(useful in business)* How did he help his friend find happiness again, after Victor's illness? *(Victor found studying the languages soothing; took a walking tour of the Ingolstadt area with him.)* What are some of the words and phrases that convey Victor's new-found happiness? *(relief, consolation, cheerfully, spirits restored, love, nature, filled me with ecstasy)*

8. How did Victor's happiness come crashing down? *(got a letter from his father saying that his little brother William had been murdered)* What is the contrast between the scene at the end of Chapter 6 and the one at the beginning of Chapter 7? *(elation/horror)*

9. Did Victor immediately suspect that the creature had killed William? *(He admitted it to himself several hours later.)* Why? *(He saw the creature during a lightning storm.)* What did he do about it? *(nothing)* What could he have done? Why didn't he tell his family what he knew? *(felt they wouldn't believe him, might blame him, couldn't catch the creature anyway)*

10. Why was Justine accused of the murder? *(The locket William had been carrying was found in her pocket.)* Did everyone think she was guilty? *(not Elizabeth or Victor)* How did Victor's father try to reassure Elizabeth? *(told her to rely on justice to protect Justine if she is innocent)* Do you think his reassurances will be born out?

Prediction
What will happen to Justine? Will she be declared innocent—or executed?

Writing Activity
You are Clerval. Write something in your journal during the time you spend nursing your friend Victor back to health. (What happened to him? How do you explain it? How are you feeling about him? What are you doing for him?)

The Author's Craft: Atmosphere
Explain that the **atmosphere** is the overall mood, the dominant emotional tone of a literary work. Atmosphere is created by the handling of setting, character, and theme. It is often described by adjectives that are used to describe the weather such as *gloomy, cheerful, threatening, tranquil*. Ask students to reread the section describing the night Frankenstein finished his creations. What is the atmosphere? *(gloomy, frightful)* How does the description of the setting contribute to that atmosphere? *("It was on a dreary night of November..." p. 42)*

Research
Find out more about the content of Coleridge's "Rime of the Ancient Mariner." Why has Mary Shelley included a passage from the poem on page 44?

Chapters 8–11

Vocabulary

infamy	obliterated	ignominious	exculpated
execrated	constrained	adduced	advocate
wantonly	timorous	bauble	ingratitude
guile	manacled	absolution	obdurate
perdition	scaffold	inexorable	hapless
unhallowed	complacency	solitude	augmenting
base	remorse	efface	abhorrence
pilgrimage	precipitated	sacrilege	tribute
depraved	benefactor	abyss	brake
access	ephemeral	guise	singular
avalanche	oblivion	barricade	imperial
pinnacle	obscure	transversely	concussion
dissipated	stupendous	aerial	recesses
gale	malignity	diabolically	dissoluble
maw	satiated	eluded	docile
clemency	community	implores	commiserate
scourge	opaque	impervious	dormant
slaked	distinguish	foliage	canopied
offals	assuage	emigration	debilitated
Pandemonium	allured	habitation	purloined
dank	meanly	incommoded	reverence
amiable	pensive	tapers	monotonous

Discussion Questions

1. What is the "incriminating" evidence against Justine? *(She was found with the locket, nor far from the body.)* Do you think such circumstantial evidence would be enough to convict her in a court today?

2. Why were many who knew Justine hesitant to come forward on her behalf? *(They assumed she was guilty, felt fear and hatred of the horrible crime.)* Do you think this ever happens today? Why didn't Elizabeth's appeal sway the crowd? *(The crowd grew even angrier that Justine could be so ungrateful as to harm good Elizabeth's brother.)* Would you say they were a bloodthirsty group?

3. Why did Justine confess her guilt? *(to obtain absolution)*

4. Victor refers to himself as the "true murderer". Why did he feel that his hands were "thrice accursed"? *(If he hadn't created the monster, William and Justine would still be alive.)* Do you agree?

5. How did Victor's father try to cheer him up after Justine's death? *(told Victor he owed it to himself and others not to grieve so much or he wouldn't be any good to anyone)* Do you agree that a mourner should try to hide his or her grief and console the living?

6. Victor says that he was tempted to kill himself after Justine's death. Why didn't he? *(This would leave Elizabeth, his father, and his other brother unprotected.)*

7. Why did Victor go to Chamounix? *(Overwhelmed by guilt and anger, he sought a place to forget his sorrows—a place he had known since boyhood.)* Do you have a place you go to when you're upset?

8. How did Victor and his creature meet up with each other? *(The creature followed Victor up a glacier.)* Why didn't Victor kill the creature, as he had imagined he would? *(The creature moved out of striking range, then pointed out that Victor had neglected him, created the creature's misery.)* Should Victor have gone ahead with his original plan, do you think?

9. How did the creature reproach his creator? *(pointed out that he is spurned by everyone; It's Victor's fault he is miserable.)* Do you sympathize with the monster? Did Victor? *(somewhat; For the first time he felt that he had duties toward the creature as his creator.)*

10. What does the creature remember about his first few weeks of life? *(He remembers darkness, fear, cold, pleasant sounds of birds, burning his hands in a fire, being attacked, finding shelter in a hovel near a cottage.)* Were these happy times for him? *(no)* Why do you think he wanted to tell his creator this tale? *(so that Victor can decide whether he owes it to the creature to help him find happiness)* Is that anything like the reason Victor has for telling Walton his story?

Prediction
How will the cottage-dwellers meet the creature? What will their reaction be?

Writing Activity
You are Frankenstein's creature. Describe the dream you have one night after watching the family in the cottage.

The Author's Craft: Suspense
Explain that suspense is a story quality that produces tension in the reader. The reader grows curious about what will happen next. Suspense usually raises one of two types of questions in a reader's mind: What will the outcome be? When will the inevitable outcome happen?

Explain that suspense created by a plot depends on (1) uncertainty about which of two opposing forces will win—or how—and (2) desire to see one force defeat the other.

Have students discuss how suspense develops in this section. (Readers wonder what the monster wants—whether he will be convinced to leave humans alone or will continue to wreak havoc; whether Victor will destroy his creation—or vice versa.)

Chapters 12–15

Vocabulary

viands	enigmatic	poignantly	ardently
perpetual	replenished	deformity	procured
arbiters	demeanor	conciliating	supple
execration	diffused	dissipates	faculty
cadence	herbage	balmy	purport
declamatory	chivalry	scion	abject
squalid	unsullied	vagabond	exhortations
sallies	affluence	consummation	tenets
immured	emulation	facilitated	meed
expostulate	tyrannical	mandate	averse
portmanteau	dejection	canvassed	pretension
disquisitions	merits	annihilation	gall
decipher	domestic	indelible	solitary
solicited	sagacity	tumultuous	endeavored
fortify	supplication	mediation	execute
irresolute	prejudiced	instigate	transport
refrained			

Discussion Questions

1. What did the family in the cottage have to be happy about? *(had each other, music, food, quiet pleasures)* Why were they sometimes unhappy? *(poor, sometimes hungry)*

2. How did the creature help the family? *(gathered wood)* Why? *(moved when he saw how the young couple gave up some of their food to the old man)*

3. What did the creature learn by watching the family? *(how to speak, read; what affection between people was like)* How do you think his life would have been different if he had wandered into the city and lived there?

4. Where did the creature live during the time he spent watching the family? *(in a hovel against the back of the cottage next to the pigsty)* How did he survive? *(gathered fruits and berries)* Was he happy? *(enjoyed the family, their music, but longed to have an affectionate relationship with someone)*

5. Who was Safie? *(the young man's girlfriend)* How did her arrival affect the family? *(cheered up Felix and the others)* How did the creature learn about world history? *(Felix instructed Safie from Ruins of Empires.)* What was his reaction to what he learned? *(horrified by details of vice and bloodshed)*

6. How did Safie's father ruin the family? *(When Felix's wealthy family defended him—a Turkish merchant condemned to death—he accepted their help; when they were imprisoned for helping him, they lost their money and he deserted them—taking Safie with him.)* Why do you suppose the author included this subplot?

7. What books did the creature first read? *(Paradise Lost, a volume of Plutarch's Lives, Sorrows of Werter)* How did they affect him? *(astonished, thrilled, depressed)* If he had been your pupil, what books would you have had him read first?

8. How did Victor's journal come into the creature's hands? *(The creature discovered papers in the clothing he had taken from Victor's laboratory.)* What effect did the journal have on him? *(He agonized as he read the details of his own creation—and how disgusted Victor was.)*

9. Why did the creature decide to present himself to the cottagers? *(He hoped that he could befriend the blind old man and through him, the younger "protectors.")* What did he hope their reaction would be? *(tolerance, at least)*

10. What moment did the creature choose to knock on the cottage door? *(when the old man was alone, playing his guitar)* Why? *(No one who could see his ugliness was home.)* What happened? *(The old man was kind to him, but Felix returned, thought his father was being assaulted, and attacked the creature in turn.)* What is ironic about the creature's choice of the word "protectors" to describe the cottagers? *(They tried to harm him.)* What do you think would have happened if the creature had tried to explain himself to Felix? Why didn't he speak—or kill Felix? *(He was sick at heart, probably had grown too fond of Felix to harm him.)*

Prediction
Where does the creature go now? What will the family do now that they have seen the creature?

Writing Activity
Felix misunderstood the creature's intentions toward the old man—and consequently beat him. Describe a time when you were treated badly by someone who misunderstood your intentions—or when you witnessed such an event.

The Author's Craft: Simile
Explain that a **simile** is a comparison that includes the words "like" or "as." For example: "Her hands are like ice cubes." Point out the simile on page 120: "I could have torn him limb from limb, as the lion rends the antelope." Explain what is being compared—and why the comparison is effective. *(The creature realizes that he had the power to kill Felix as easily as a lion kills his prey; this comparison conveys the creature's power, Felix's naïveté, and the fact that the creature feels the natural instinct of self-preservation—but feels no malice toward his potential victim.)*

Chapters 16–19

Vocabulary

glutted	impotence	myriads	retreat
imprudently	irretrievable	appeased	tenement
combustibles	vestige	succour	redress
visage	imprecate	respite	imbibed
epithets	malignity	atone	requisition
concede	abject	feint	manifested
undulations	siroc	haggard	disquisition
proportionably	eradicating	salutations	conjure
avow	exordium	infirmities	coveted
enfranchised	intimated	machinations	sedulous
bourne	picturesque	inaccessible	variegated
promontory	meandering	populous	chastened
cataract	replete	blight	dejected
allusion	novelties	insolent	gratification
elasticity	debasing	repose	superscription
expedite	remissness	languid	compensated
dissuade	barren	persecutor	obscure

Discussion Questions

1. The creature asks, "Why, in that instant, did I not extinguish the spark of existence which you had so wantonly bestowed?" (p. 121) Does this remind you of something someone else has said? *(Victor talked about considering suicide.)* Why didn't the creature kill himself? *(He wanted to get revenge.)*

2. How did the creature spend the days after leaving the cottagers? *(wandering in the woods)* How did he try to "mend the damage" at first? *(He returned to the cottage to talk to the old man.)* What did he learn when he returned to the cottage? *(The family had decided to quit the cottage because they felt they were in danger.)*

3. How did the creature's feelings change when he learned that the cottagers were gone? *(despair)* What drove him from that point on? *(revenge and hatred)* What plan did he make? *(burned the cottage, resolved to go to Geneva and find his creator)* Would things have been different if he had found the family in their home?

4. What did the creature do when the girl fell in the water? *(pulled her out, tried to help)* Why, do you think? Did this surprise you? How did the creature get shot? *(The young man who tore the girl from the creature's arms shot him when he followed.)*

5. What do we learn from the creature's tale about how William died? *(He seized the boy, hoping to befriend him; when the boy struggled and revealed who he was, the creature grew angry and decided to get revenge through the boy.)* What was the creature's intention at first? *(to make friends and educate someone who was a blank slate)* Does this remind you of Victor's intention in creating the creature? Why did the creature kill the boy? *(vengeance)*

6. Why did the creature put the locket in Justine's dress? *(to make her suffer as he presumed she would make him suffer by reacting in disgust if she had awakened and seen him)* What do you think would have happened if she had awakened?

7. What demand did the creature make? *(He wanted Victor to create a mate.)* Why did Victor refuse at first—then agree to the plan? *(At first he thought that he might be creating another source of wickedness; then he reconsidered and felt that he owed the creature a companion.)* What pros and cons did he consider? What else should he have considered?

Should I make a female?

Reasons Yes	Reasons No

8. Victor's father noticed that he was feeling glum. What did he think was the problem? *(that perhaps Victor did not want to marry Elizabeth)* How did he feel about Elizabeth and Victor marrying? *(The father wanted that union.)* Why did Victor put off the wedding? *(He wanted to follow through on his promise to the creature before enjoying his own marriage—otherwise he might endanger his family.)*

9. Why was Victor worried about leaving his friends and going to London? *(They wouldn't know the danger they were in.)* Do you think he should have warned them? Why didn't he? *(He figured the creature would follow him.)*

10. How did Clerval end up traveling with Victor? *(Victor's father encouraged Clerval to keep Victor company.)* What parts of their journey stick out in your mind? Why did they separate? *(Victor told Clerval that he wanted to tour Scotland alone because he wanted his friend to enjoy himself—but didn't feel up to socializing with strangers.)*

Prediction

What will happen when the creature finds that the scientist is making a female, as requested?

Writing Activity

Victor has parted from his friend, Clerval. Write one postcard that Victor might have sent his friend.

The Author's Craft: Foreshadowing

Explain that **foreshadowing** is a hint or suggestion of something that will happen later in a story. Ask students what they think is being foreshadowed by the last line on page 149:

> "I looked toward its [the female's] completion with a tremulous and eager hope, which I dared not trust myself to question but which was intermixed with obscure forebodings of evil that made my heart sicken in its bosom."

Chapters 20–22

Vocabulary

unremitting	malignant	compact	provocation
propagated	sophisms	arrested	presentiment
heaths	vice	gnashed	requited
grovel	insatiate	barbarously	insuperable
fiend	oppressive	basest	prelude
sanguinary	reverie	breakers	mutable
debility	inhospitably	magistrate	politic
calamity	ignominy	supposition	apothecary
convulsions	affright	apparatus	turnkeys
livid	renowned	abode	precarious
relapse	assizes	vexations	languishing
paroxysms	vigilance	inquietude	laudanum
repose	delirium	deranged	obliterate
imperious	dictate	paradisiacal	enunciation
conduce	adversary	consecrate	emaciated
omnipotent	invincible	prophetic	tangible
artifice	solemnization	presentiment	nuptial
emulate	insurmountable	fluctuating	amphitheatre

Discussion Questions

1. Why did Victor destroy the female creature? *(He saw the malice on the creature's face and realized that he might be creating another instrument for evil.)* Do you think he should have followed through on his promise to the creature? What threat did the creature make, in return? *("I shall be with you on your wedding night.")* Why didn't Victor kill the first creature, too? *(The creature eluded him, jumping into a boat.)*

2. What did Victor do with the remains of the female? *(put them in a basket and threw it over the side of the boat into the water)* Why? *(He didn't want the peasants to be horrified/suspicious.)* What else could he have done?

3. How did Victor find out about Clerval's death? *(He was accused of the death by some Irishmen.)* Why was he suspected? *(Some recognized his boat as the one that had been seen near the scene of the crime.)* What was his response? *(He fell into a fever again, raving that he was a murderer.)*

4. Why wasn't Frankenstein executed? *(The magistrate took a liking to him; witnesses came forth to say that he was elsewhere when the body was found.)* Do you think he would have been better off if he had died?

5. Why did Frankenstein's father think that his mind had been deranged? *(His son had nightmares, talked of monsters, murder.)* What would have happened if Victor had explained why he felt that he was a murderer?

6. Why did Elizabeth write to Victor? *(She was giving him an "out" in case he no longer wanted to marry her.)* Are you surprised that she still cared about him after the way he had treated her? Would you write such a selfless, supportive letter if you were in her shoes?

7. Why did Victor decide to marry Elizabeth? *(He figured that if he delayed, the creature would only take more lives.)* What did Victor think the creature's threat meant? *(that the creature would kill Victor)* Are you surprised that he didn't worry more about Elizabeth's safety?

8. Where did Victor and Elizabeth plan to honeymoon? *(Villa Lavenza–Italy)* What did Victor promise to tell Elizabeth the day after they were married? *(his dark secret)* What do you think she would have said if he had told her the truth before the marriage? Why do you suppose he didn't plan to tell her immediately after they were married? Did he really think he'd be around the day after?

9. How did Victor feel as the wedding approached? *(strangely tranquil)* Why wasn't he more worried? *(It seemed as if the threat were a delusion; also, he felt that finally his destiny would be decided.)* How do you suppose the creature was feeling as the wedding date drew near?

10. How did Elizabeth feel as the wedding approached? Can you explain why? *(She had a presentiment of something evil.)*

Prediction
Why does the day of the wedding present to Victor "the last moments of my life during which I enjoyed the feeling of happiness"? What happens after the wedding?

Writing Activity
Victor had promised to confide his tale to Elizabeth the day after their wedding. Suppose he had decided to gather his thoughts first by jotting down what he would say. Write his notes and the tale he planned to tell.

The Author's Craft: Verisimilitude
Explain that **verisimilitude** is the quality of the story which gives it the appearance of being momentarily true—no matter how far-fetched. Ask students to point out in this section of the story details which give this highly improbable story **verisimilitude**. (e.g., The description of the creature's "howl of devilish despair" and later his threat, "I shall be with you on your wedding night" convey the arguably natural disappointment and anger the creature experienced when he realized he would not get what he wanted—a mate.)

Chapters 23–24

Vocabulary

bier	acme	tedious	vacancy
vales	habitation	reconciled	resource
delirium	wont	adjuration	repast
impassive	perseverance	invigorated	unabated
gibe	sledge	intercept	hamlet
retribution	protraction	disencumbered	appalling
succour	asseverations	mutilated	communion
imposing	auguries	mutiny	deputation
stigma	modulated	paramount	actuated
irradiation	portend	repentance	superfluous
hypocritical	opprobrium	contumely	conflagration

Discussion Questions

1. Victor expected the creature to attack. Why, then, did he send his wife off alone to bed? *(He didn't want her to be upset by the attack on him.)* What do you think would have happened if he had stayed with her?

2. How did Elizabeth die? *(The creature strangled her.)* Why do you suppose the author didn't choose to describe the actual murder?

3. Why did Victor decide to go right back to Geneva after the murder? *(He worried about the safety of his father and brother.)* Do you think this was the best plan? He said, "no creature had ever been so miserable as I was". Do you sympathize with him—or do you think he is whining a little self-pityingly?

4. How did Victor's father die? *(He was distraught about Elizabeth's death and died shortly after learning of it.)* Why do you suppose Shelley didn't have the creature murder him—as he does in the Kenneth Branagh film version?

5. What plan did Victor make regarding the creature? *(to pursue him to the farthest ends of the earth if necessary and kill him)* Was it a good one? Why did he decide to tell the magistrate the tale—when he hadn't told it before? *(He hoped that the authorities could help apprehend the murderer.)* What do you suppose were Victor's exact words? Did the magistrate believe him? *(Victor felt not.)*

6. Why did Victor go to the graveyard? *(to promise his murdered friends that he would avenge their deaths)* Why did the creature whisper that he was "satisfied"? *(Now he knew that Victor was determined to live.)*

7. How was Victor able to follow the creature—where? What kinds of clues did he find? *(The creature left marks on trees, stones—even messages; Victor followed him to the North country.)* Why did the creature leave these clues? *(Victor assumed that he was being tormented; maybe the creature also wanted Victor's company.)*

8. Before he died, what did Victor make Walton promise? *(that he would kill the creature)* Why? *(so that the creature couldn't hurt anyone else)* Did Walton follow through on that promise? *(no)* Do you think Victor would have killed the creature as he planned, had he lived? Alternatively, do you think the creature would have killed Victor, had Victor been alive when the creature arrived on the scene?

9. How did Victor die? *(After telling Walton to seek happiness in tranquility, he simply slipped away.)* Are you surprised by the creature's response to Victor's death? *(The creature holds his creator, mourns his death, asks his pardon.)* He tells Walton that Walton didn't get the whole story from Victor. *("...But in the detail which he gave you of them he could not sum up the hours and months of misery which I endured..." p. 204)* What do you think about the creature's suffering? What do you think happened to the creature after he was "lost in darkness and distance"?

10. What advice did Victor give Walton about continuing his journey northward? Was this good advice? *(Victor told Walton's men to remain steady to their purpose; once Walton assured them that they would return to England, Victor told Walton he had given up his purpose.)* Why did Walton decide not to continue on? *(Walton decided he couldn't lead his men unwillingly into danger.)* Do you think Walton's decision was influenced in any way by the tale Victor told him? *(Victor had related the horror of feeling responsible for the deaths of others, something Walton may have decided he wanted to avoid.)*

Post-reading Extension Activities

Post-reading Discussion Questions

1. How did you feel after reading *Frankenstein*? Hairs on the back of your neck still prickling? An unsettled feeling? Satisfied? Down? According to Aristotle, representations of suffering and death in literature paradoxically leave the audience feeling relieved rather than depressed. Does this hold true for you after reading this story?

2. Why do you suppose Mary Shelley does not show us the death of the creature at the end? Is there a chance that he lives on—or that a sequel was planned?

3. Before reading the novel, you probably had many ideas about the story from what you'd seen on TV, at the movies, in comics, etc. Did the novel surprise you in any way?

4. How did you feel about the creature? about Victor Frankenstein? Which character(s) in the story did you want to protect?

5. What questions would you like to ask Victor Frankenstein? the creature?

6. At what points in the story do you think the scientist made the most important decisions? Which of these do you feel were the right decisions?

7. Why do you suppose Mary Shelley gave the creature no name—but we popularly refer to him as "Frankenstein"?

8. Here are some criteria ("measuring sticks") for a good horror story:
   - horrifies us by bringing us to dark places in the mind
   - describes a foe who is cruel/uncontrollable
   - draws on our disgust

   What do you think of these criteria? Would you change or add any? Does *Frankenstein* meet these criteria? If so, how? If not, how would you change the story to make it better? If you viewed a film version of the story—Do you think the changes made the story better?

9. With what other stories, poems, plays, movies would you group this one? Did the creature remind you of other characters you have met in literature or film? What does he have in common, say, with the Hunchback of Notre Dame or the Elephant Man?

10. Reread the statements you considered in the anticipation guide (prereading activity #1 or Activity #1 in the Student Packet). Discuss/write about these in light of the novel you have just read.

Suggested Further Reading

Early gothic/horror stories:
Smollett—*Ferdinand Count Fathom*, 1753
Horace Walpole—*Castle of Otranto*, 1764
William Beckford—*Vathek, an Arabian Tale*, 1786
Anne Radcliffe—*The Mysteries of Udolpho*, 1789-1797

Gothic romances—by Matthew Lewis, William Godwin, Charles Brockden Brown

Poetry that has felt the Gothic influence:
Coleridge's *Christabel* and *Kubla Khan*
Wordsworth's *Guilt and Sorrow*
Byron's *Giaour*
Keats' *Eve of St. Agnes*

Horror classics:
Robert Louis Stevenson's *Dr. Jekyll and Mr. Hyde*
Robert Louis Stevenson's *The Body Snatcher and Other Stories*
Short stories by Hawthorne and Poe
Daphne du Maurier's *Rebecca* (a novel without the Gothic setting but with a brooding atmosphere and sense of unknown terror)
Jane Austen's *Northanger Abbey* (a spoof of stories with a "damsel in distress" in a terrifying locale)

Contemporary horror stories:
Stephen King's *Four Past Midnight* and *Misery*
Martin Valerie's *Mary Reilly*
Ruth Riddell's *Shadow Witch*
John Saul's *Creature*
Earle Westcott's *Winter Wolves*
Daniel Cohen's *Southern Fried Rat and Other Gruesome Tales*
Joan Aiken's *Give Yourself a Fright: Thirteen Tales of the Supernatural*
L. M. Montgomery's *Among the Shadows: Tales from the Darker Side*
Books by R. L. Stine, Lois Duncan, and Joan Lowery Nixon

Viewing

View two film versions of the story. (The 1931 classic black and white with Boris Karloff as the Monster is considered one of the greatest horror films ever made.) Compare them with each other—and with the novel. How was the storyline changed? Did you feel more or less sympathetic toward the creature in the movie than toward the one in Shelley's novel? Was the novel more or less "moralistic" in tone than the movie? Is Shelley's "message" about scientific advance the same as the movie director's?

Writing

Letter: Pretend that Victor and Elizabeth have exchanged birthday presents. Write the thank-you notes that they send each other.

Newspaper Article: Write an objective account of one of the events in the story, such as the execution of Justine. Include eyewitness reports and quotations.

Poem: Write a poem in response to the novel. It might be
- a "Once/then" poem from Victor's point of view.
- a prayer-poem by Justine
- a diamente showing how the creature changes
- a list poem detailing the parts from which the creature was made
- a poem of apology by Victor
- a love poem from Victor to Elizabeth
- a bitterness poem by the creature
- a poem that ends with a line taken from the story (e.g., the creature's words on finding his master dead: "Oh, Frankenstein! Generous and self-devoted being!")

Short Story: Read in the Preface about how Mary Shelley came to write the short story upon which her novel is based. Pretend that you were in that circle of friends, sitting around the fire. Write your own horror story. Include some of the elements that are commonly found in stories from the gothic genre (an atmosphere of brooding and unknown terror, emphasis on story instead of character delineation, abundance of horrors). For some excellent horror story "recipes" that walk you through how to write your story, see Karen Hubert's *Teaching and Writing Popular Fiction* (Teachers & Writers Collaborative, © 1976).

Alternative Ending: Replace the creature's final scene (heading to the North, apparently to die) with another scene from your imagination.

Movie Review: Review one of the film versions of the story. Include a brief summary of the story, evaluate changes made in the original, tell what you thought of the casting, and give an overall thumbs up or thumbs down.

Diary Entries: Write accounts of an incident in the story from two perspectives (e.g., Elizabeth's thoughts about why Victor has grown so distant and Victor's thoughts during the estrangement).

Dream Diary: Assume the point of view of one of the characters (e.g., Victor, the creature, Elizabeth) and describe three dreams that you have during the course of the story.

Flashback: Write a flashback to a time before the start of the story—for example, a scene from Victor's childhood in which his interest in science is already evident.

Therapist's Report: You are Freud. Victor Frankenstein (or the creature) comes to you and tells you his troubles. Write a brief case study describing your patient—and conclude with at least three recommendations.

Place: Write a description of a place mentioned in the story, such as the inside of the cottage. Flesh out details provided by Shelley with those supplied by your imagination.

Screenplay: Pretend that you are the writer of a *Frankenstein* video production, working on the final death scene. You have decided to use a series of dissolving images to show the memories that pass through Victor's mind as he fades away. Describe the images.

Add a Scene: We never actually "see" what happened to Elizabeth in the end. Describe her final encounter with the creature, or write a few pages describing another event which is mentioned but not fully described (i.e., Justine's execution).

Essay
1. Read the legend of Prometheus. Why do you think Shelley entitles her novel *Frankenstein—or—The Modern Prometheus*?
   (Have students research the myth first or provide this information: In Greek mythology, Prometheus is the fire-giver. Also known as "forethought," he created man to gaze at the stars, gave man reason and obtained fire from the sun for man's comfort. His brother "afterthought," on the other hand, created animals to turn their eyes on Earth. Zeus got upset with Prometheus for being so devoted to humans, and had him chained to a rock in the Caucasus, where an eagle eats his liver forever.)
2. Shelley uses a passage from *Paradise Lost* as the epigraph for her work (See page xii of *Frankenstein*—Bantam paperback.) Find out more about *Paradise Lost*. What are the parallels between Milton's work and Shelley's?
3. The idea of giving birth is a recurrent motif throughout *Frankenstein*. Do some research on Mary Shelley's life. Trace the births and birth images found in the book, describe the atmosphere that surrounds them, and speculate about how Mary Shelley's real-life experiences may have contributed to these scenes.
4. Write an essay that answers this question:
   Was Victor Frankenstein a victim? You might find it helpful to use the notes you made for prereading activity #11 as supportive evidence for your opinion. Also, you might consider these questions in your answer: Why did Frankenstein create the creature? At what points—if any—could the scientist have prevented the deaths of his friends? Could Victor have been a better "parent" to the creature? What—if anything—does Victor's advice to the captain show that Victor has learned?
5. Write an essay that answers this question: **Was the creature evil?** You might find it helpful to refer to the notes you made for prereading activity #12 in writing your answer. Also consider these questions: Why did the creature kill his victim, in each case? Did he feel remorse? Why did he want a female? Why did he head north, at the end?
6. Compare and contrast Victor with his friend, Clerval.
7. Explore the idea that the fiendish creation is actually Victor's counterpart—a representation of his dual nature.

8. Trace the theme of corruption throughout the play. Who is corrupted? How? What is Mary Shelley saying about our society? How is she commenting on the impact of scientific discovery?
9. Respond to the following statement by Sir Arthur Conan Doyle, using your own response to the novel, *Frankenstein,* either to support or refute it: "**Where there is no imagination there is no horror.**"

Listening/Speaking

Interview
Have the class interview students playing the roles of Victor, Elizabeth, Clerval, and the creature. (Students come up with at least three questions each for homework. For example: "Victor, why did you want to do these experiments, anyway?" or "Clerval—why did you make friends with Victor?")

Debate
Hold a classroom debate on the following question: **Was Frankenstein's creature evil?**

Students who argue "yes" get on one side of the room. Students who argue "no" get on the other. Both sides try to convince the "undecided" students, who remain in the middle.

Mock Talk Show
Pretend that Oprah Winfrey is doing a show on "people with dark secrets." Victor appears as a guest, along with two or three other characters from literature (such as Dr. Jekyll, the werewolf, the phantom of the opera). Have Oprah and the audience members ask these characters about their experiences—what their secrets are, why they tried to keep these matters secret for so long, how these secrets have affected their loved ones, etc.

Drama
1. Divide into groups for a class presentation of four or five scenes from the novel. Create simple props (e.g., a locket to be found with Justine; a guitar for the old man in the cottage) and costumes (e.g., a lab coat for Victor; a wedding veil for Elizabeth).
2. Write and act out a scene that was mentioned but not shown (e.g., the murder of Victor's little brother).
3. Write and act out a scene that didn't happen in the novel—but might have. For example, show what might have happened if
   - Victor had tried from the first to be a "good father."
   - Elizabeth had discovered what Victor was up to.
   - Victor had given the creature a female.
   - The creature had found Victor in the end before Victor's death.
4. Recast your favorite scene as a radio play and record it on tape—complete with sound effects and music.
5. Select a scene and stage a "tableau" (actors frozen in place). (For example, how would the scene where the creature looks in on the cottagers look?)

Language Study
1. Choose a line from the story that particularly sticks out in your mind for some reason. Read it aloud to your group and discuss how Shelley uses sounds, images, contrast, etc., to create a memorable effect.
2. List your favorite similes and metaphors in the novel.
3. List the 20 vocabulary words you think any reader of this novel should know—and why.
4. List 20 words used by Shelley that are "dated" now—and provide the contemporary equivalents.

Art
1. Create your own version of the monster as you imagine him—using paints, markers, papier mâché, collage—any medium you like.
2. Choose the scene in *Frankenstein* that you think you will remember longest and reproduce it as a six-frame cartoon strip. (Fold a long piece of paper into six panels; use balloons for dialogue.)

Music
1. What music was popular at the turn of the century? What tunes might Victor Frankenstein have hummed while he worked on his creation?
2. What is your favorite scene in the story? What music would you use to capture the mood of that scene? What do you think of the background music you heard in the film version(s) of *Frankenstein* that you viewed?
3. Write a song about one of the characters in *Frankenstein* and set it to a well-known tune (e.g., "Clementine").
4. Write a ballad about the doomed love of Victor for Elizabeth. Set it to a tune from a well-known ballad, such as "Barbara Allen."

Research
1. Find out about:
   - "reanimation" experiments that were actually being done around the time that Mary Shelley wrote the novel.
   - laws and regulations that scientists in this country are currently bound by when they experiment on human beings (e.g., genetic engineering, use of fetal tissue in research, rights of human subjects).
   - the Industrial Revolution. (What was it? During Mary Shelley's lifetime, how did it affect the way many people made a living? What social upheavals did it bring? What happened to the sick and the elderly?)

2. Create a colorful timeline to show actual events that the author might have included in the story, supposedly occurring at the turn of the 19th century (such as the War of 1812, Grimm's fairy tales, Lamarck's "Philosophie Zoologique," etc.).